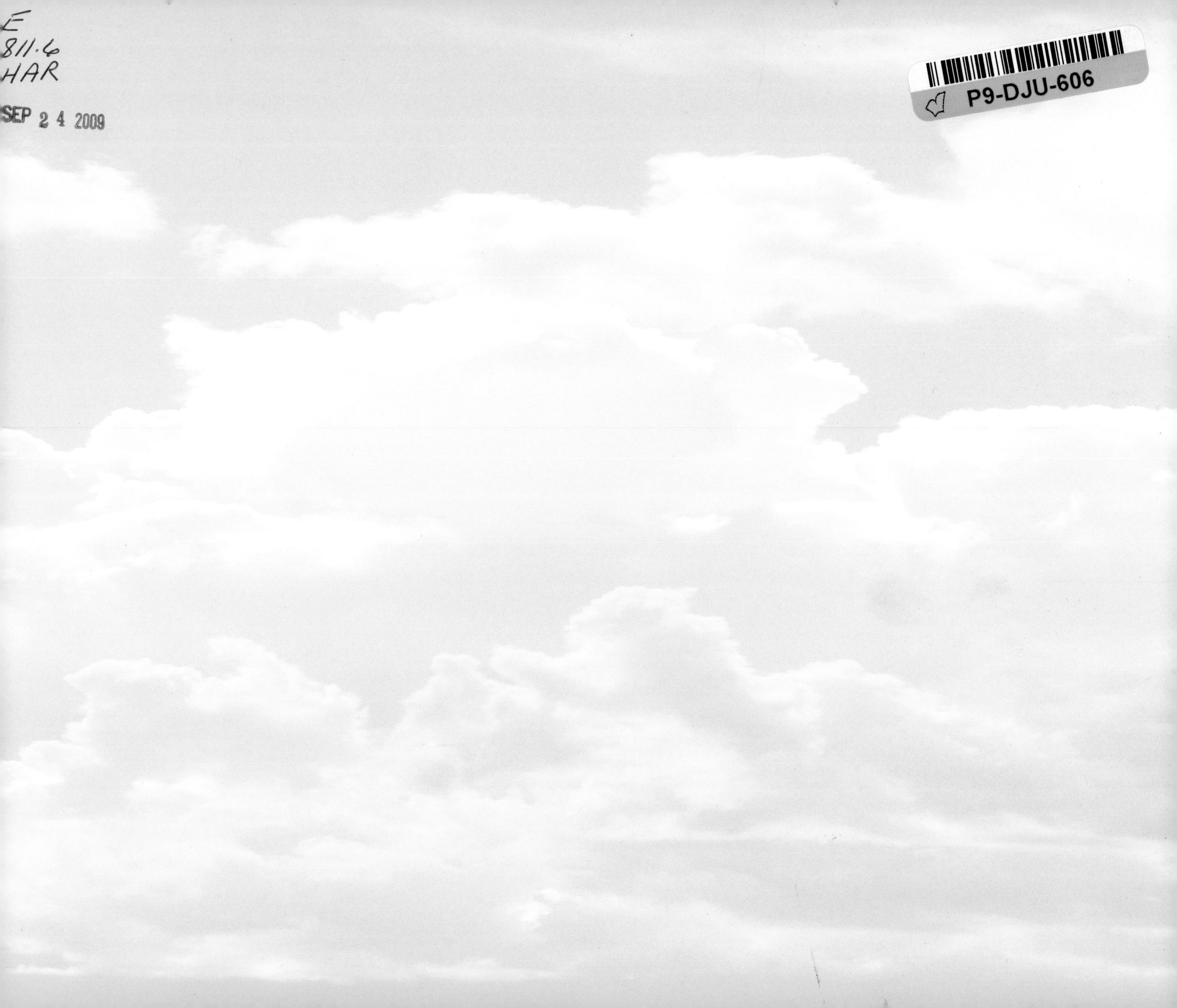

African Acrostics

A WORD IN EDGEWAYS

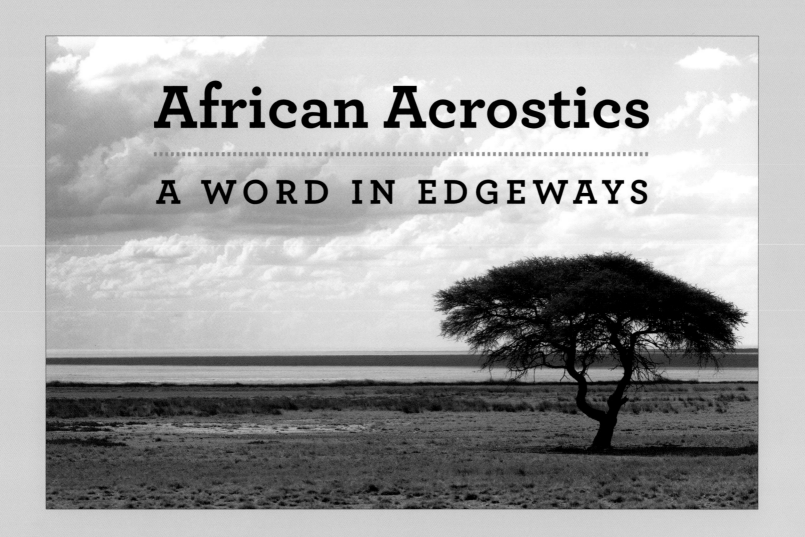

poems *by* **Avis Harley**   photographs *by* **Deborah Noyes**

CANDLEWICK PRESS

With special thanks to Jane and Chris

A. H.

For Kasha, Tim, Laurel, Meine, Gina, and Tomás

D. N.

Text copyright © 2009 by Avis Harley
Photographs copyright © 2009 by Deborah Noyes

First edition 2009

Library of Congress Cataloging-in-Publication Data
Harley, Avis.
African acrostics / Avis Harley ; photographs by Deborah Noyes. — 1st ed.
p. cm.
ISBN 978-0-7636-3621-0
1. Animals — Africa — Juvenile poetry. 2. Children's poetry, Canadian. 3. Acrostics. I. Noyes, Deborah, ill. II. Title.
PR9199.3.H345A69 2009   811'.6 — dc22
2008017916

2 4 6 8 10 9 7 5 3 1

Printed in China

This book was typeset in Archer.

Candlewick Press
99 Dover Street
Somerville, Massachusetts 02144

visit us at www.candlewick.com

ACROSTIC (uh-KROS-tik)

Welcome, all poets—both new
Or well versed. Non-rhymers or
Rhymers! Come,
Dive in headfirst!

Inviting all writers—
Now you're just the right age.

Explore the acrostic that rides
Down the page.
Get a word you
Enjoy and would like to define.
Write it down vertically
And fill in each line.
Your name is a very good way to begin.
Surprise yourself. Find that poem within!

A Croc Acrostic

Crackerjack-attacker
Reptile-in-my-dream
Old-mythmaker
Carnivore-supreme
Open-opportunist
Dragon-eye-agleam
Inner-grinner
Lizard-wizard
Enemy-extreme!

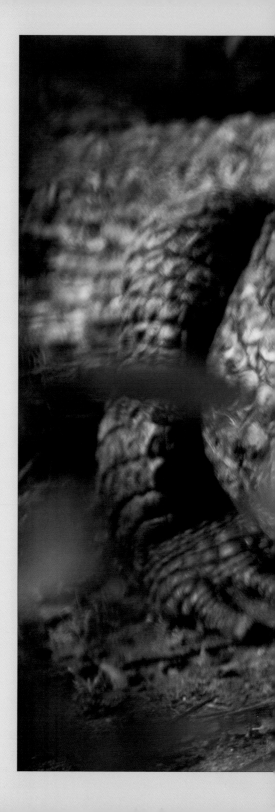

Moody Guy

Boulders for shoulders,
Elegant horn —
A pointed reminder of the
Unicorn,
Thick leg-pillars bruising tawny
Yellow grass

In huge hide shoes,
Nobody argues

This is a colossal
Holdover from
Earth's primeval swamp.

But
Even so, I know
A rhino when I
See one, and this is the time not
To.

Kudu Kudos

How do you do a "How-do-you-do" if
Ever you meet a kudu?
Reach out
And shake hand with a horn curlicue? Or
Loudly holler a hearty "Halloo!" Whatever you
Do, kudu kudos is due.

Your Majesty

Lion looks so lazy, watching day-life pass,
Yet searing eyes are stalking shadows in the grass.
Inside a mighty golden throat, he stores his
Nightmare roar that sends his subjects
Galloping across the sunstruck floor.

Hornbill's Hot Day

Marvel at this splendid scarlet wattle-bib
Underneath my squawker of a bill! I
Think today is too warm to utter
Even one word of bird . . .

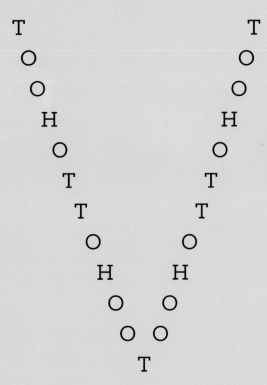

Eye to Eye

Ear-sails flap in a breeze.
Leather limbs in rhythm
Evenly swaying in step
Plod slowly over Africa.
Huge as a dinosaur, yet
A tender soul from such
Noble mammoth alumni.
There is wonder abuzz,
Staring into eyes so wise.

Skysweepers

Orange beaks are
Unique with their bill-clacking rackets
That attract other
Storks in
Those black
And white jackets. But when
Night steals across and
Daylight is done, storks keep
In their beaks a
Nip of
Gold sun.

Untamed

What
Interest have zebras in
Leather tethers or
Dusty saddles?

Since only
The wind
Reins
In their
Power, and sun so
Easily
Straddles.

Above All

Celebrate these
Long-standing giraffes,
Opening
Up clouds and eaves-
Dropping on the wind!

Far
Removed
In airy
Elegance,
Nibbling on high, they
Decorate the
Sky.

Buffalo Bluff

When you meet with a buffalo fellow
And you feel your legs turn into Jell-O,
  Though your fear is acute,
  Calmly say to the brute,
"Hello, you great beast of a bellow!"

  Foolish you if you ask for a ride:
  Ugly thoughts might lie under his hide
(Like he charges too much).
  Lest his mind-set is such,
  You are better off stepping aside.

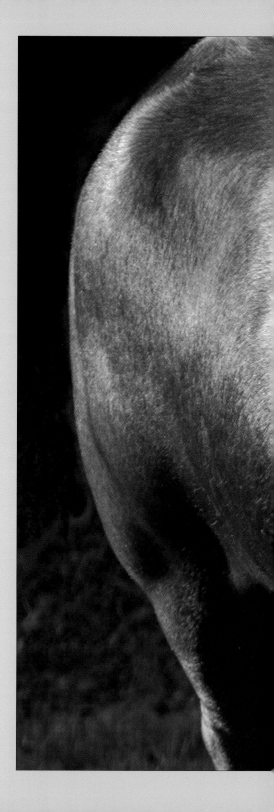

Now Listen to Me, Son

First, my fowl,
Avoid all humans, who only come
To gawk and giggle. They
Hanker for our ostrich plumes and
Envy how our swan-necks wiggle.
Really! Have you seen those people-toes?
Little tiny things in rows! How they
Yearn for ones we've got: so down-to-earth,

And second, esteem your lot.
Drink in the
View! Wear lofty airs!
Implant upon your brow a scowl.
Colored feathers? Well, who cares —
Enjoy the gifts you've got, my fowl.

The Watcher

Silent sits the slinker.
Oh, wise, intelligent thinker!

Morning on
Earth's warming hearth, awash in
Lazy spill. Does *my* cat dream of
Leaping kin
On our sunny
Windowsill?

Lookout

Lightning locked
In legs of plush velvet.
Old Nobility poised:
Noiseless.
Even
Sunlight
Shivers.

Bonobos Know

Parents the world
Over
Plainly know: back-
Packing your young is the
Easy way
To go.

Impalas in Peril

Every	reflex	wired to	escape	ambush,
Yet	elegant	heads	are	aware,
Each	attuned	and	reading	Africa,
Sensing	dangers	trespass	soft	still air.

Sipping the Sunset

Rooting around
In the Zambezi—river life looks
Very easy, slurping down an
Evening drink, then
Rolling in luscious mud to sink

Right into delicious squish—what more could
Ever a hippo wish? Faithful birds
Vacuum the hide and
Efficient fish clean teeth inside.
Rich is the life that lazes
In sun, *but* . . . if
Ever you see a hippo run—RUN!

Wild Whispers

Bat-eared fox and wind
In the stalks are
Given to conversation.

Ears such
As these can
Read any breeze, even
Sound out punctuation!

Leopard Plan

Pass over a
  branch under
  moonlit sky.
    Slowly. Though
      still and quiet
      blanket the night,
        quieter still am I.

MORE ABOUT ACROSTICS

The acrostic is a playful poetic form that people have enjoyed writing and reading since ancient times. The name comes from *akros,* the Greek word meaning outermost, or end, and *stichos,* meaning row, or a line of verse. Although the form has many variations, the most popular is the traditional acrostic, in which the first letters of the lines, when read downward, spell a word or words. Using a personal name is an easy way to start writing an acrostic. Here's one about my lionhearted cat, Sockeye:

Somehow I know
Our old
Cat
Keeps sly secrets behind those
Enormous
Yellow
Eyes.

Most of the acrostics in this book contain a vertical word or message in the first letters of the line, but two of the poems are *double* acrostics, in which the first letters *and last* letters in each line contain a message when read downward:

Cats that wash their paws and pur**r**
Across your lap are deceiving yo**u**:
They are dreaming of Roar and Prow**l**,
Shadowing through the jungle hu**e**.

An even more challenging variation is the *multiple* acrostic, as in the poem "Impalas in Peril," which contains *five* vertical arrangements. (Look carefully!)

Yet another variation on the form is the *cross* acrostic, in which the hidden word is read in a step pattern: the first letter of the first line, the second letter of the second line, and so on down through the poem:

Chin
w**a**shed, Sockeye
  si**t**s in the morning sun,
   whi**s**kers of a lion twitching.

The poem "Hornbill's Hot Day" is both a concrete poem and an acrostic. The slanted message is read downward *and then* upward. And there, the shape of the slanted lines themselves adds to the poem's meaning.

Acrostics offer the writer an intriguing framework for a poem, and single acrostics are not difficult to create. Think of a word, phrase, or even a whole sentence that catches your imagination. Then write it vertically. You can use one word per line, or many words—rhymed or unrhymed. A predetermined letter can sometimes spark an unexpected idea, and it's great fun to hide a word or message for your readers!

Astonish yourself—
Create a poem that
Reads
On its
Side.
Think of the fun when
It lets the letters help you
Choose.

NATURE NOTES

CROCODILE

This heavily armored African reptile can grow as long as 16 feet (4.87 meters). Swimming with only its nostrils and bulging eyes showing, the crocodile has long jaws that do not even ripple the surface as it stalks prey. Crocodiles sometimes get close enough to shore to snatch land animals — even humans — and drag them back into the water.

RHINOCEROS

The rhino loves to wallow in water, roll in mud, and sometimes feed neck-deep among swampy plants. Its small eyes aren't too useful, but it possesses an amazing sense of smell. This bulky beast is not fat but bulging with muscle.

KUDU

Kudus are antelopes and, like impalas, are grazers and browsers. During the day, they remain under dense cover, and they feed mainly in the early evening hours. Kudus are handsome creatures, and the males have magnificent spiraled horns.

LION

King of the Beasts! This big cat with the thunderous roar once roamed freely over parts of Europe. The lion's mane of shaggy fur makes him look even larger and more intimidating than he is. It also helps to protect his head by cushioning blows in battle. Lions patrol their territory and guard the females. They feed on animals that graze, especially zebras and wildebeests.

HORNBILL

The southern ground hornbill is deserving of its name, so bizarre is its beak! It is a large, prehistoric-looking bird. Instead of hopping

along the ground, it walks, making strange grunting and booming sounds when its bright red neck wattle is inflated. The hornbill eats fruit but also hunts live prey, such as insects, lizards, and even hares.

ELEPHANT

Elephants have wonderful memories. They are very intelligent animals and have been known to grieve when a member of the herd dies. The elephant's two tusks are actually extra-long teeth; the longest tusk ever recorded was more than 11 feet (over 3 meters) long. The elephant's heavy trunk is in fact its nose.

STORK

A migrating stork on its journey to winter in South Africa can fly as high as 16,000 feet (4,875 meters). The stork is known as one of the long-legged "glamour birds." Its long neck acts like a periscope, allowing it to peer above tall marsh grasses. A stork communicates with a castanet-like sound made by the rattling of its beak.

ZEBRA

Plains zebras roam the open grasslands like wild horses. Baby zebras, called foals, are very friendly and playful. They chase one another, often racing around with young gazelles and antelope. Each zebra has a slightly different pattern of stripes, like our unique fingerprints.

GIRAFFE

The giraffe is the tallest land animal, and its neck makes up one third of its height. The tallest giraffe ever measured was 19.3 feet (5.9 meters) in height. To feed its huge body, a giraffe must spend sixteen to twenty hours a day browsing shrubs and trees. Giraffes do not have leaders in their small herds, and they are very social creatures.

BUFFALO

If provoked, the African or Cape buffalo is a fierce attacker with formidable horns. But mostly it likes to graze on grasses. Buffalo like to live near water—for drinking as well as for escaping biting insects. They are the wild cattle of Africa, and their herds can number a thousand or more animals.

OSTRICH

The ostrich lays the world's largest bird egg. It can equal the weight of thirty hens' eggs. Newly-born ostriches can run almost as soon as they are hatched. They love to explore and flee the nest as soon as they can. The ostrich is a spectacular runner—in fact, it is the fastest two-legged racer on earth! It can gallop along at 40 miles per hour (64 km/h).

AFRICAN WILDCAT

As early as 3500 BC, the Egyptians began domesticating small cats when they discovered that the African wildcat was saving their vital grain stores from rats and mice. This feline is a probable ancestor of today's house pet and is very similar in appearance and size to our tabby cat.

LIONESS

If you watch your pet cat stalk and pounce, it is hunting just the way a lioness does. Keen eyesight and hearing, razor-sharp claws and teeth, and fast reflexes make the lioness an expert hunter. Even though lionesses do most of the hunting, the male eats first. Of all the big cats, lions are the only ones that live in groups, called prides.

BONOBO

Bonobos are long-limbed, chimpanzee-like apes that give their babies lots of love and are wonderful parents. They are intelligent and have a very sensitive nature. Scientists studying a bonobo in captivity have been able to teach him to "talk" using keyboard symbols. Young bonobos love to make funny faces and are very playful. Female bonobos are in charge of their communities, despite being smaller than the males.

IMPALA

The impala is a graceful antelope, a slender, deerlike mammal. It can make the most astonishing leaps when startled, sometimes as much as 9 feet (2.74 meters) vertically, or more than 30 feet (9.14 meters) horizontally. It nibbles on grass and browses on tender leaves.

HIPPOPOTAMUS

Hippopotamus means "river horse." The huge hippo is at home in the water and can be submerged for four minutes before having to surface for air. In the evening, it lumbers onshore to eat grass and other vegetation. When the hippo yawns, it is displaying fearsome tusk weaponry. The yawn is a threat that may start a serious fight with another hippo.

BAT-EARED FOX

The bat-eared fox is a member of the dog family. Its extra-long ears allow heat to escape and help the animal keep cool. It is a night hunter and mostly feeds on insects.

LEOPARD

Tucked up in the branches of a tall tree, the leopard is in an ideal place to snooze, survey the land, or pounce on prey. The leopard is a solitary hunter and can drag fairly large animals back up into the tree, thus keeping its prey from other carnivores. This cat has a distinctive pattern of black spots, many of which have caramel-colored inner spots.

A NOTE FROM THE PHOTOGRAPHER

Most of the animals in this book—excluding water species like hippos, crocodiles, and one or two others—were photographed in game parks and preserves in Namibia, a dry country in southern Africa.

I took hundreds of photos in Etosha National Park, one of Africa's oldest and largest reserves, in Namibia's northwest Kunene Region. Countless species—among them elephants, zebras, lions, leopards, cheetahs, rhinos, and numerous antelope—visit the water holes of Etosha. Driving along the park's seemingly endless gravel roads, we scattered herds of impala and saw giraffes nibbling at spiky acacia by the roadside. One especially fortunate day, we glimpsed a mother ostrich herding chicks and idled a long while (with the engine running) just a few feet from a male lion drowsing under a tree.

People in Namibia spend a lot of time waiting for and measuring rainfall. One of my most vivid memories was of standing at Etosha's Okaukuejo (a water hole where you can leave your vehicle) at twilight while a dramatic thunderstorm rolled in. With clouds banked high, literally towering against a vast skyline, a family of giraffes with bowed heads—still miles away—made its languid way in for a drink. I could smell the slanting rain long before it hit, and *just* before, a storm of beetles came pinging in with the winds.

There is a lot of sky in Namibia, a near-endless horizon, and a gazillion stars at night.

Outside Etosha, with wise guides, I tracked a rhino on foot and a cheetah and leopard by Jeep. But I spent much of my time (hours at a time, really) alone in a fiberglass termite mound—or swaddled in camouflage in a makeshift photographer's blind in the V of a tree—sweaty and stooped (and, in one case, tick-bitten) to spy on kudu, jackals, and warthogs near small water holes. I loved every minute of it.

Pebble™ Plus

Under the Sea

Sea Horses

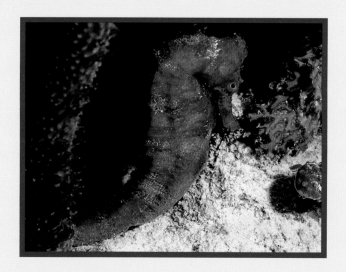

by Carol K. Lindeen

Consulting Editor: Gail Saunders-Smith, PhD

Consultant: Jody Rake, Member
Southwest Marine/Aquatic Educators' Association

Capstone
press

Mankato, Minnesota

Pebble Plus is published by Capstone Press,
151 Good Counsel Drive, P.O. Box 669, Mankato, Minnesota 56002.
www.capstonepress.com

1 2 3 4 5 6 10 09 08 07 06 05

Library of Congress Cataloging-in-Publication Data
Lindeen, Carol K., 1976–
    Sea horses / by Carol K. Lindeen.
    p. cm.—(Pebble Plus—Under the Sea)
    Includes bibliographical references and index.
    ISBN 0-7368-3662-4 (hardcover)
    1. Sea horses—Juvenile literature. I. Title. II. Series.
QL638.S9L56 2005
597'.6798—dc22   2004011099

Summary: Simple text and photographs present sea horses, their body parts, and their behavior.

Editorial Credits
Martha E. H. Rustad, editor; Juliette Peters, set designer; Kate Opseth, book designer; Kelly Garvin,
    photo researcher; Scott Thoms, photo editor

Photo Credits
Bruce Coleman Inc./Masa Ushioda, 8–9
Corbis RF/Marty Snyderman, 1; Amos Nachoum, 6–7
Herb Segars, cover
Minden Pictures/Birgitte Wilms, 10–11; Fred Bavendam, 18–19; Norbert Wu, 14–15, 20–21
Seapics.com/Bob Cranston, 4–5; Lines Jr./Shedd Aquarium, 12–13; Rudie Kuiter, 16–17

Note to Parents and Teachers

The Under the Sea set supports national science standards related to the diversity
and unity of life. This book describes and illustrates sea horses. The images support
early readers in understanding the text. The repetition of words and phrases helps early
readers learn new words. This book also introduces early readers to subject-specific
vocabulary words, which are defined in the Glossary section. Early readers may need
assistance to read some words and to use the Table of Contents, Glossary, Read More,
Internet Sites, and Index sections of the book.

Table of Contents

What Are Sea Horses? 4

Body Parts 8

What Sea Horses Do 16

Under the Sea 20

Glossary 22

Read More 23

Internet Sites 23

Index 24

What Are Sea Horses?

Sea horses are fish.

5

Sea horses are about
as long as a new pencil.

Body Parts

The head of a sea horse
looks like the head
of a horse.

Bony plates cover sea horses.

The plates help keep

sea horses safe.

plate

Sea horses have fins.

They move their fins to swim.

fin

Sea horses have curly tails.

They hold on to plants

with their tails.

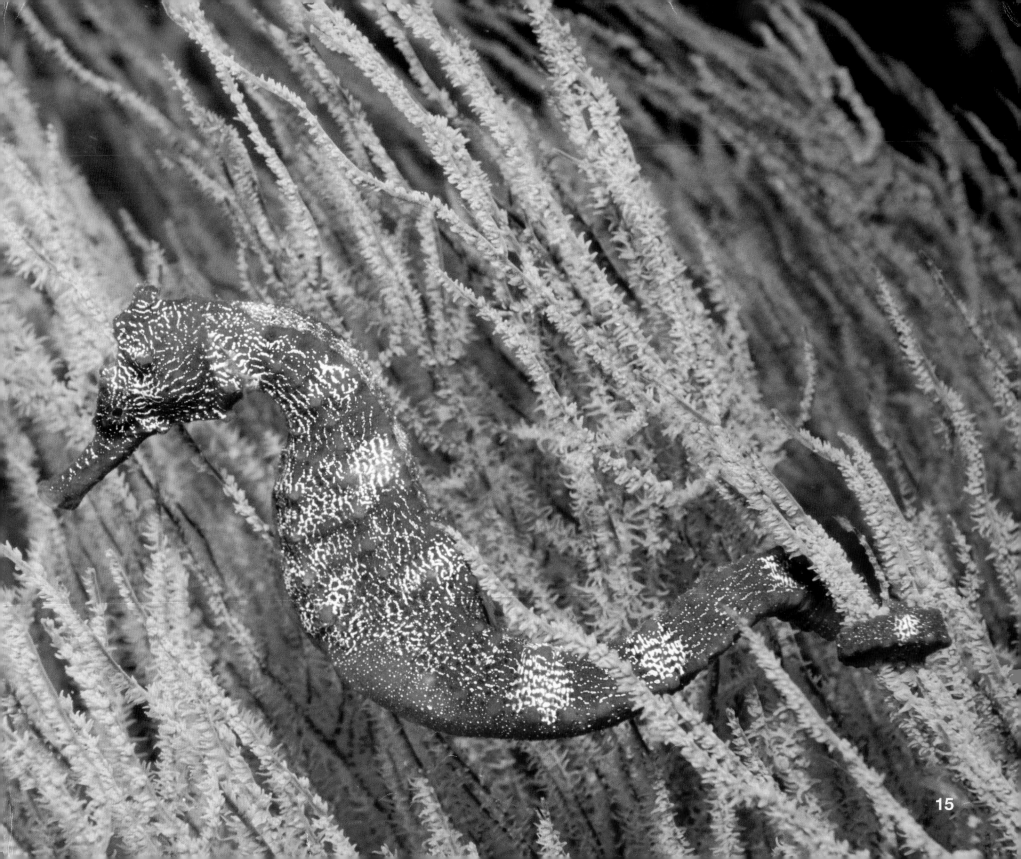

What Sea Horses Do

Sea horses hold on

to each other

with their tails.

Sea horses can change color.

They hide near plants.

Under the Sea

Sea horses swim

in shallow water

under the sea.

Glossary

bony—hard like a bone

curly—curved or twisted

fin—a body part that fish use to swim and steer in water

fish—a cold-blooded animal that lives in water and has fins and gills

plate—a hard covering on an animal's body that helps keep it safe

shallow—not very deep

Read More

James, Sylvia M. *Seahorses.* New York: Mondo, 2002.

Jango-Cohen, Judith. *Clinging Sea Horses.* Pull Ahead Books. Minneapolis: Lerner, 2001.

Longenecker, Theresa. *Who Grows Up in the Ocean?* Who Grows Up Here? Minneapolis: Picture Window Books, 2003.

Internet Sites

FactHound offers a safe, fun way to find Internet sites related to this book. All of the sites on FactHound have been researched by our staff.

Here's how:

1. Visit *www.facthound.com*

2. Type in this special code **0736836624** for age-appropriate sites. Or enter a search word related to this book for a more general search.

3. Click on the **Fetch It** button.

FactHound will fetch the best sites for you!

Index

change color, 18

fins, 12

fish, 4

habitat, 20

head, 8

hide, 18

plants, 14, 18

plates, 10

shallow, 20

size, 6

swim, 12, 20

tails, 14, 16

Word Count: 90
Grade Level: 1
Early-Intervention Level: 9